This book belongs to:

_____

_____

ISBN: 9781709476334
Copyright © 2019 Tim Bird.

All rights reserved. No part of this publication may be reproduced, distributed, or transmitted in any form or by any means, including photocopying, recording, or other electronic or mechanical methods, without the prior written permission of the publisher.

The contents of this book are believed to be correct at time of printing. Nevertheless the publisher cannot accept responsibility for errors and omissions, changes in the detail given or for any expense or loss thereby caused.

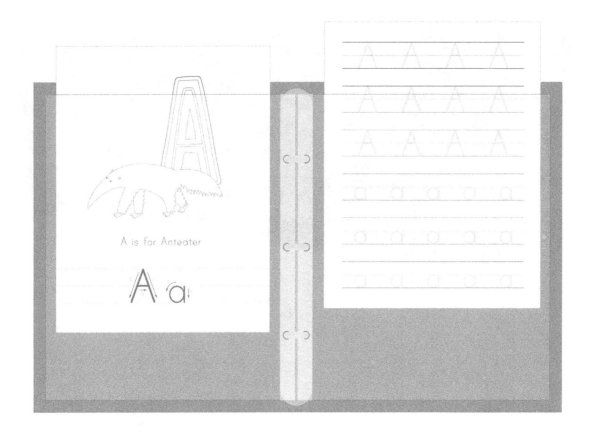

Non permanent/dry wipe-clean pen

Why not try this?

This is a great way to get the most out of your book...

1. Cut out the pages from the book.

2. Slide them into clear plastic sleeves and put in a ring binder.

3. Trace over the letters using a non permanent/dry wipe-clean pen.

4. When finished wipe off your letters and start over!

Technique

1. Rest the pen on your middle finger: A. and the area between your index finger and thumb: B.

2. Pinch the end of the pen/pencil with your index finger: C. and thumb: D.

3. Relax your hand and follow the arrows to trace the letter.

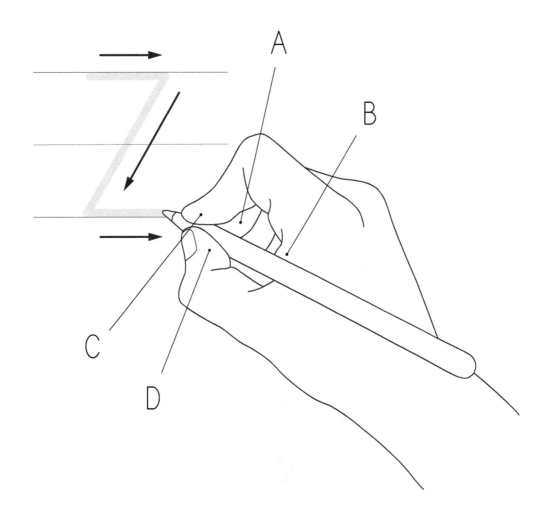

A is for Anteater

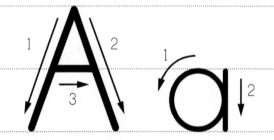

B is for Beaver

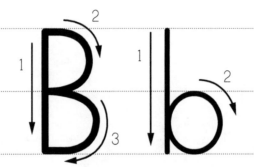

C is for Chameleon

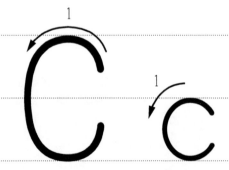

D is for Dolphin

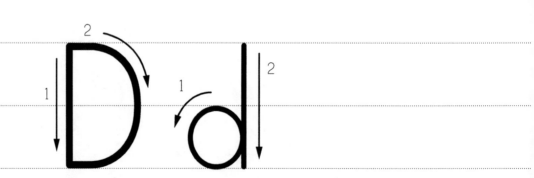

E is for Eagle

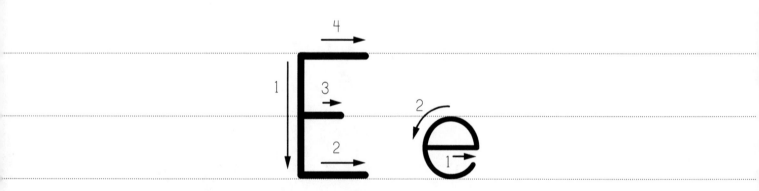

F is for Flamingo

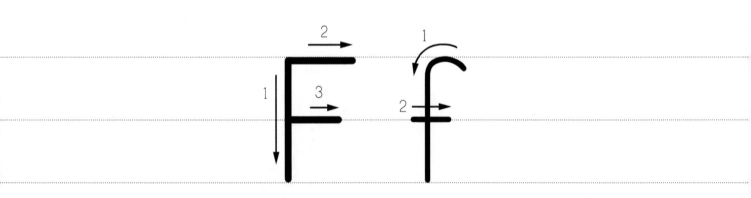

G is for Gorilla

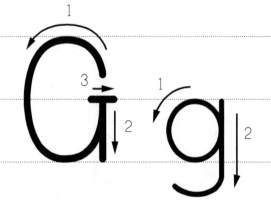

g g g g g

g g g g g

g g g g g

g g g g g

g g g g g

g g g g g

H is for Hedgehog

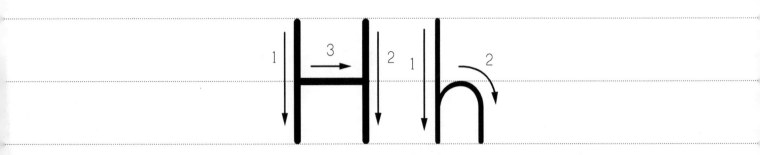

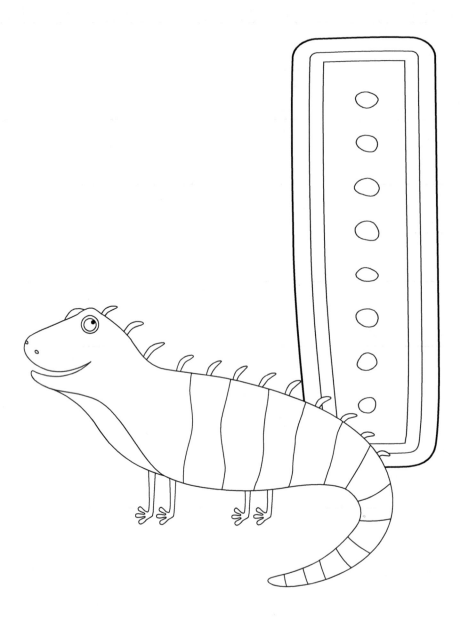

I is for Iguana

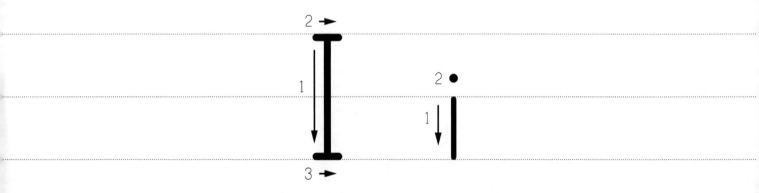

J is for Jaguar

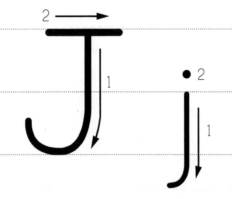

K is for Kangaroo

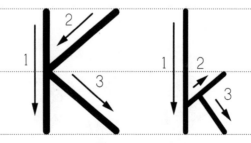

L is for Lemur

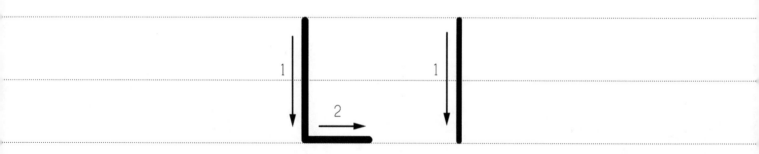

M is for Manta

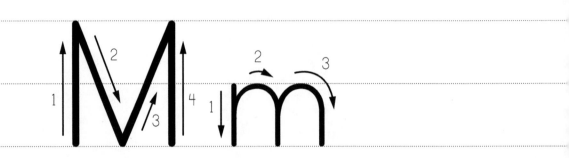

N is for Numbat

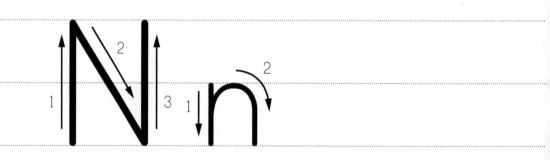

O is for Ostrich

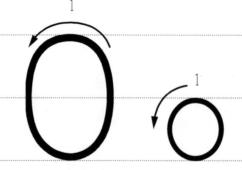

P is for Pelican

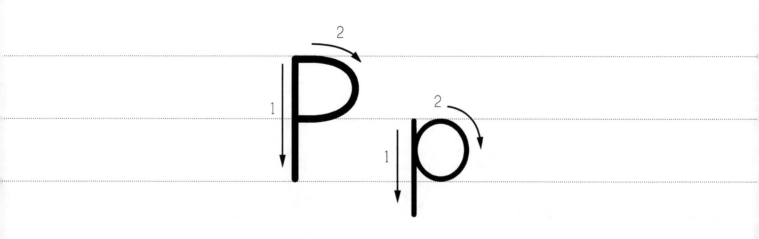

p p p p p

p p p p p

p p p p p

p p p p p

p p p p p

Q is for Quail

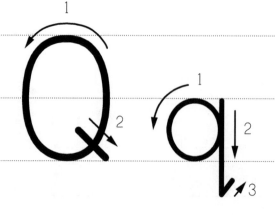

R is for Rat

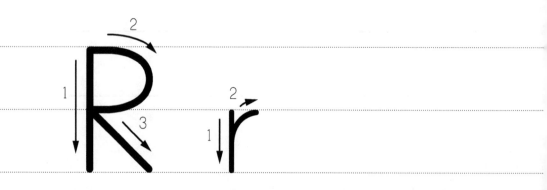

R R R R

R R R R

R R R R

r r r r

r r r r

S is for Squirrel

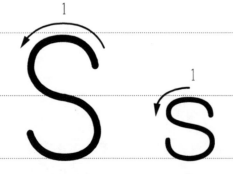

T is for Tortoise

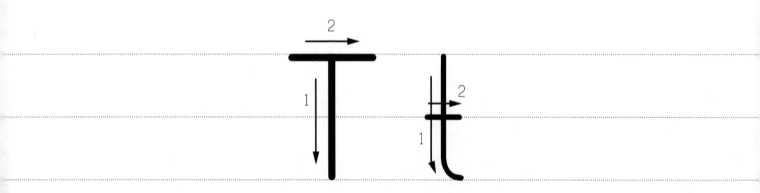

U is for Uguisu

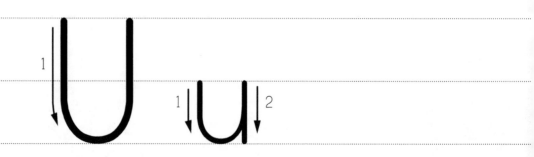

V is for Vulture

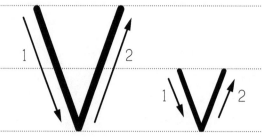

W is for Walrus

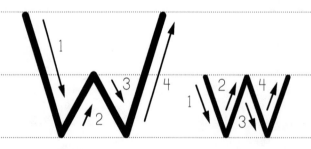

X is for Xantus

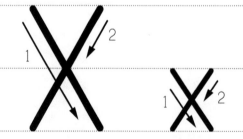

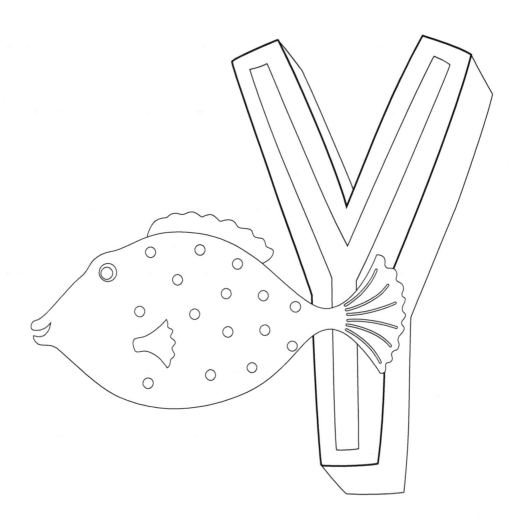

Y is for Yellowfish

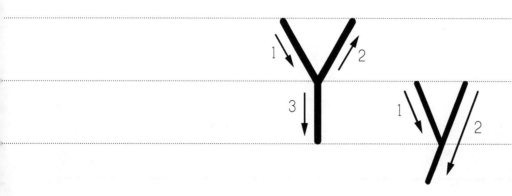

Z is for Zebra Bird

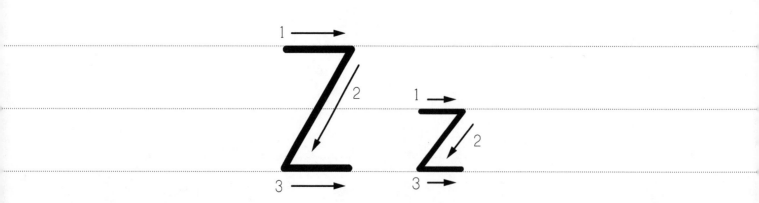

Congratulations - You've done it!!!

The rest of the book contains blank pages for some more practice...
oh, and a certificate of achievement at the back to fill in!

Did you like this book?

If you did then would you please consider leaving me some positive feedback on Amazon? It will help so much and allow me to continue making more books like this one.

Thank you!

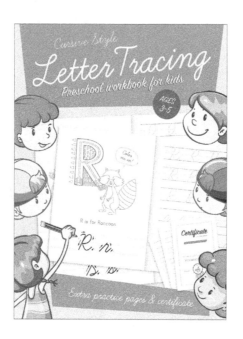

Be sure to check out
Cursive Style Letter Tracing!

Available exclusively on Amazon -
just type in the ISBN: 9781709479670
in the Amazon search bar.

Certificate

OF ACHIEVEMENT

THIS CERTIFICATE IS PROUDLY PRESENTED TO

For Mastering your 'Plain Style' ABC

Congratulations on completing the Plain Style Letter Tracing book!
It's such a major milestone & now you're ready to put it to good use!

SIGNATURE   DATE

Printed in the USA
CPSIA information can be obtained
at www.ICGtesting.com
LVHW062201190924
791626LV00038B/806